Nutcracker Art

30 Nifty Nutcrackers for Coloring

Scott Cummins

OUTSIDE-THE-LINES.COM

Outside-the-Lines.com

OutsideTheLines.com

Outside-the-Lines.com

Outside-the-Lines.com

Outside-the-Lines.com

OutSide-the-Lines.com

Outside-the-Lines.com

Outside-the-Lines.com

Outside-the-Lines.com

Outside-the-lines.com

Outside-the-Lines.com

Outside-the-Lines.com

Outside-the-Lines.com

OutSide-the-Lines.com

Outside-the-Lines.com

Printed in Great Britain
by Amazon